# WOMEN LIVING FOR JESUS IN VICTORY

Lauren D. Triplett

Diligence Publishing Company
Bloomfield, New Jersey

All rights reserved.

Copyright © 2021 by Lauren D. Triplett

This book or no parts of this book may be reproduced, transmitted in any form by any means (electronic, photocopy, recording or otherwise) without the written permission of the author.

All scripture quotations are taken from the New King James Version (NKJV) and the King James Version (KJV) of the Bible.

First published in Greensboro, North Carolina. Printed in the United States of America, 2021

Cover design: Ashley Marshall

Cover photo: Gloria Spinks

ISBN: 978-1-7374840-4-2

# DEDICATION

This book is dedicated to my Lord, Savior, and King, Jesus Christ, Son of the Living God. My life experiences with God are what have encouraged and enabled me to write this book. He is the reason for all of my joy, peace, and happiness. He is the reason that I even exist. I want Him to receive all the glory, honor, and praise for this book because He is worthy.

# TABLE OF CONTENTS

Introduction ........................................................................ 1
1. How To Give Your Life To Jesus Christ ...................... 9
2. Who Am I Now? ............................................................ 17
3. How To Experience A Spiritual Birth In Jesus Christ ... 23
4. Characteristics of A Godly Woman ............................. 37
5. Characteristics of A Godly Wife .................................. 43
6. Characteristics of A Godly Mother .............................. 57
7. Conclusion .................................................................... 73
About The Author ............................................................. 75
Order And Contact Information ....................................... 79

# ACKNOWLEDGEMENTS

To my husband, Milton Triplett, and our three sons, Jason, Jonathan, and James. You all are truly a precious gift from God to me. I love and appreciate you all with all my heart. My sincere thanks for always encouraging me to do whatever God is telling me to do. Thank you for always giving me your love, prayer, support, and inspiration to be able to write and become the author that God has purposed for me to be.

To my spiritual father in the gospel who definitely has a shepherd's heart, Pastor Michael Thomas. Thank you for teaching and preaching the true unadulterated Word of God. You have been an encouragement and guidance to me to write this book. Under the power of the Holy Spirit, you have been an inspiration to me as you lead by example on how to live a life that is pleasing to God. Also, under your teachings, you are equipping men and women of God to do what God has called them to do.

To my church family at Love and Faith Christian Fellowship. Thank you for all the love, prayers, and support that you have shown my husband and I since we joined the church in June, 2012. Under the guidance of the Holy Spirit, we are all growing together with the grace and knowledge of God as a unified front to do what God has called us to do for His glory and for our good.

To Jim Murray and the "Write It Right Editorial Services" team. I appreciate and thank you for your patience, guidance, and direction in helping me to write this book. Since this is my first time ever attempting to write a book, your professionalism and expertise as my editor have been beyond my expectations. May God's blessings and favor continue to be upon you.

To Pastor Rebecca Simmons and Diligence Publishing Company. Thank you for all the time, effort, patience, and the excellence shown in publishing this book, *Women Living for Jesus in Victory,* and bringing it into manifestation. May God continue to bless you and Diligence Publishing Company because you are a blessing.

To the rest of my family, loved ones, and friends, know that you all have been an encouragement and inspiration in some way to me in writing this book, *Women Living for Jesus in Victory*. Love you and may God bless and keep you all in His care.

# FOREWORD

*Women Living for Jesus in Victory* is a must-read. In chapter after chapter, Lauren Triplett has outlined a very detailed path. The outline that is given in this book shows how to apply godly principles through the Word of God to our daily living as Christian women. You will learn who God has made you to be as well as know your purpose here on earth as you walk with Him every day. As a wife and mother, she has explained what you are to do and how you are to do it; by reading, worshipping, and having a godly lifestyle.

*Women Living for Jesus in Victory* is a wonderful book for beginning your life as a woman of God. Living in victory is the most rewarding life you can have in the Christian community. As you read this book, it will give you step by step the instructions you need to move progressively. In each chapter, Lauren Triplett gives you important directions to go in through the Word of God; from the point of salvation and then to knowing who God has made you to be.

My experiences with her have ensured me that she has been confirmed by God and recognized by man to be one of the most anointed people in the Kingdom of God. I thank God every time I think about what she has taught me on how to become a godly wife, mother, and friend and how just to know who I am and not let others define me. So, you must read this book to enrich your life with God and beyond that.

I have known Lauren Triplett for over 20 years. She is my mother in the Spirit. She is an intercessor anointed by God. She used to tell me that I was going to be an author, and by the grace of God, I have written two books as well as music and poetry. She has prayed me through many hard times and places. She has always been there for me even after my own mother passed away. That is how I know that the words she has written in this book will bless your life.

*Regina Hughes*

# Women Living for Jesus
# In Victory Defined

**WOMEN:** The nature, characteristics, or feelings often attributed to women; womanliness.

**LIVING:** In actual existence or use.

**FOR:** Intended to belong to or be used in connection with.

**JESUS:** Also called Jesus Christ. He's the Son of God. Our Savior, Lord and King! He died on the cross for our sins.

**IN:** Used to indicate transition from one state to another. Used to indicate object or purpose.

**VICTORY:** A success or superior position achieved against any opponent, opposition, and difficulty.

(Source: Online Dictionary)

# Women You Are Called To Victory

## *Women Living for Jesus In Victory Mission Statement*

Striving and learning how to live the life of Christ with victory and purpose. We have been delivered and set free through the blood that was shed on the cross by our Lord and Savior Jesus Christ. Therefore, as Women of God, we no longer have to live a defeated life as a victim, but as a victor!

***1 Corinthians 15:57 (NKJV)***
*57 "But thanks be to God, who gives us the victory through our Lord Jesus Christ."*

***Proverbs 31:10 (KJV)***
*10 "Who can find a virtuous woman? For her price is far above rubies."*

# INTRODUCTION

Before sharing how women can live for Jesus in victory, I want you to know how *Women Living for Jesus in Victory* came into existence. In 1993, I stopped working for corporate America, got licensed by the State of Michigan and opened up a daycare in my home. Our three sons were very young at the time so I could only be licensed to care for six children, which included our three sons. I wanted to do this because our children were so young, and my husband agreed with me. Not only were our children very young, but we thought it would be best if I would be at home to take care of them. Also, daycare expense was almost taking all of my monthly income that I received from my job.

I never had a lot of children in the daycare. Our three sons and another three or less children were enough for me to take care of by myself. I only had the daycare for about a year and a half. I found out that God had a plan for me that I wasn't even expecting that would branch off from the daycare.

One of the parents in particular started bringing their daughter for me to care for while they both had to work. I noticed with the mother that something was really troubling her. My past experiences of abuse made me want to reach out to her with love and compassion. I never asked her what she was going through. In other words, God gave me wisdom on what I should and shouldn't say to her. We became friends, and she started opening up to me allowing me to minister to her. She told me that she was being abused by her husband. I would pray with and for her. As I was led by the Holy Spirit, I would share scriptures from the Bible with her. I never tried to take the place of God in her life. I knew that God wanted me to lead her to Him. She even started going to our church. She started growing and maturing in God and His Word.

One day, she approached me with these words, "Lauren, you are always encouraging me with the Word of God and praying for me. I've told a couple of my friends about you. What do

## INTRODUCTION

you think about having Bible study and prayer with some women here in your home?"

Needless to say, I didn't feel comfortable with what she asked me at all. I was just fine with God using me on a one-on-one basis with people.

You see, I had been very badly hurt by my family, friends, and in churches. I still had trust issues. I was ordained as an evangelist at this little storefront church when I was in my twenties. From there, under the guidance of the Holy Spirit, I was preaching and teaching the Word of God. I give all the glory, honor, and praise to God. It was none of me and all of Him. When I met her and started my daycare, I was in my forties. That is at least 20 years after I had gotten ordained as an evangelist. I started asking myself, *"What in the world made her even want to ask me something like that?"*

Well, feeling that way didn't last very long at all. God got with me and reminded me, with so much love, who He was and whom I belonged to. He reminded me that He saved me for such a time as this. My life was not my own, and I belonged to Him. It was then that I knew that God was taking me out of my comfort zone.

I talked it over with my husband, and he showed me love, compassion, and support and prayed for me. He always encourages me to do whatever God leads me to do. I told her that I had prayed about it and I would do it. So, my home daycare was brought to a close. I was led by the Holy Spirit to talk to our pastor, at the church we were attending at that time, about what I was about to do. He said he would pray for me and gave me encouraging words.

One day, before I started the ministry in my home for women, I heard God tell me to call the ministry "Women Living for Jesus in Victory."

I was nervous about meeting this new task that God had given to me. I told God how much I needed Him. He reassured me that He has never left or forsaken me, and He wasn't about to do it then.

The Lord had His way and women were healed, delivered, and set free right in my home. God's Word says in Matthew 18:20, where two or three are gathered together in His name that He would be in the midst of them.

God kept His Word. We never focused on how many attended or didn't attend. We just allowed the Holy Spirit to have His way, and He

## INTRODUCTION

did. What is so awesome about God birthing this ministry, "Women Living for Jesus in Victory," through me, is that I was being healed, delivered, and set free right along with the women that came to my home once a week. All of this from a daycare that I started in my home. Thank you, Jesus. My King of Kings and Lord of Lords.

God told me years ago to know the seasons that He has me in. You know, seasons do change. "Women Living for Jesus in Victory" was a blessing in so many ways. God brought a closure to that ministry and started me back to ministering to people in the Body of Christ (the churches). The last time I talked to the woman that was being abused by her husband and brought her child to my daycare, she had given me a praise report. I'd rather not mention her name, but she got a divorce from her husband, received a certificate from Bible school, was a prayer warrior and was president over the usher board at the church she was attending at that time. Praise God!

I'm still a work in progress. God is not finished with me yet. In fact, God is not finished with any of us yet. This life journey that God has me on helped me to realize that I had to die to myself (my old way of thinking and living), deny myself, pick up my cross, and follow after Jesus. I also had to realize that I couldn't do it successfully or victoriously without Him. God's grace is sufficient for me, and His strength is made perfect even in my weakness. The day that I got saved and gave my life to Jesus Christ, I found joy unspeakable and full of glory.

Unfortunately, I found out that after you get saved, the change for the better doesn't happen overnight. It is a process, and it takes time. I had to get rid of my old self so the new creation in Christ Jesus could come forth. I couldn't understand why I was still going through some of the same things I was going through before I got saved. I love God, and I knew when I got saved that He loved me. Not knowing any better, I thought as a babe in Christ, that because God saved and loved me, that it meant that all my griefs and sorrows would go away.

I learned in studying God's Word that if I continued to obey His Word and put my faith and trust in Him, then there would be nothing too hard or impossible with Him. I never gave up wanting to live for the Lord, please Him, and show Him how much I loved Him. I thank God for loving me and never leaving and forsaking me. I thank God for being on this journey of life with me so I can reach the destiny and purpose that He has planned for me for His glory.

There is nothing new under the sun. I pray that as you read this book, *Women Living for Jesus in Victory*, that you begin a life-changing experience with the Lord. I pray that as you read this book, that you will find the peace of God which surpasses all understanding, that will keep your heart and mind in Christ Jesus. I pray that in this book you will discover just how much God really loves and cares for you. I'm praying and believing God that as you read this book, you will experience your journey of being delivered and set free from your past; that you will become a new creation in Christ Jesus. Old things will pass away, and all things will become brand new for you in your life. I pray that after reading this book, you will become a victor and no longer a victim so that you will be able to reach your destiny and purpose in God.

# CHAPTER 1

## *How To Give Your Life To Jesus Christ*

I was raised in a house with just my father, mother, sister, and me. My sister and I were also raised in church. My mother had my father take us to church every Sunday; but he didn't want to go. As a little girl, church was confusing for me to hear what was being preached and taught from the Bible.

One example involved a young woman named Mary, a virgin whose unborn child was conceived by the Holy Spirit. After she gave birth to her child, He was named Jesus. As He grew up, some people started acknowledging Him as Jesus Christ, the Son of God. Jesus, who knew no sin, lived, ministered to mankind, was crucified, and shed His blood on the cross for the remission of our sins. He died, was buried, and rose again on the third day with all power and authority in His hands.

As a little girl, the Word being preached was beyond my understanding. Of course, I would ask questions, but still didn't get the answers to help me to better understand this man named Jesus. I became devastated when I started hearing that Jesus was nailed to a rugged cross when He did no wrong. I would literally cry, especially when I heard how they hammered nails through His hands and feet. They even pierced Jesus in His side with a sword! I couldn't understand how people would do such a horrible thing to somebody that was innocent of what they were accusing this man Jesus of. I would ponder in my young mind, *"If Jesus didn't do anything wrong, why did they do this horrific thing to Him?"*

Again, I was just a little girl, and hearing what they did was overwhelming to me. I really couldn't understand that after Jesus was crucified on the cross, he died and was buried and that He rose from the dead three days after He was buried. You know little children hear about ghosts. So hearing about that was very scary to me.

I never stopped wondering why Jesus would allow people to falsely accuse Him of something that He didn't do. After the false accusations, they continued to spit, mock, and beat Him to the point that He didn't even look human. Then, they nailed Him to the cross after doing all of that to Him. I found out as time went on why Jesus allowed that to happen to Him.

When I got older and moved out of the house I was raised in, I started attending other churches. I felt more fulfillment in understanding God's Word in the churches that God had me to attend. As I started to hear the gospel preached, which is the good news, I began to get a better understanding of how God loved me so much that He gave His only begotten Son, Jesus, to die on the cross for my sins. You see, I didn't understand when I was a little girl about what God did for me and why.

I had to grow up and experience a life filled with hurt and pain to understand why God wrapped Himself up in flesh and was born through the virgin Mary. He lived, died, and rose on the third day so that I would have an opportunity to believe in Him and live a more victorious and abundant life as His child. In doing so, I could get healed, delivered, and set free from my sins so I could live with God for all eternity. Even though it was challenging for me to let go of my past hurts and pains, I heard the gospel and I was willing to give my life to Jesus Christ. He gave His life on the cross for my sins, so why shouldn't I give my life to Him? I wanted to show Jesus just how much I loved Him for loving me first. The more I surrendered my life to Him, the more He turned my messes into messages and my tests into testimonies!

God didn't do all of this just for me but for you too. He never promised that it would be easy after you give your life to Jesus Christ. However, Jesus promised us that in Him, we will have peace, no matter what trials and tribulations we are going through.

To give your life to Christ, you must first know just how much God really loves you. After you confess with your mouth and believe in the birth, life, death, and resurrection of our Lord and Savior Jesus Christ, then that is the beginning of you experiencing a new victorious life. You must let go of past hurts, pains, unforgiveness, bitterness, strife, or anything that is contrary to God and His Word. You have to be willing to let go of your old way of living, thinking, and believing. You have to be transformed by the renewing of your mind. You do this by continuing to pray, fast, read, study, and hear the Word of God. Reaching the goals and destiny that God has for you takes time. It is a process that you must be willing to go through, knowing that while you are on this new journey with Jesus Christ, you are not alone. He promised to never leave or forsake you. So let go and let God be in control of your life.

As stated by Pastor Michael Thomas at Love and Faith Christian Fellowship Church, "You are not just going through, but you are growing through!"

### *John 16:33 (NKJV)*
*33 "These things I have spoken to you, that in Me you may have peace. In the world you will have tribulation; but be of good cheer, I have overcome the world."*

### *John 3:16 (NKJV)*
*16 "For God so loved the world that He gave His only begotten Son, that whoever believes in Him should not perish but have everlasting life."*

### Romans 10:9, 10, 13 (NKJV)

9 "that if you confess with your mouth the Lord Jesus and believe in your heart that God has raised Him from the dead, you will be saved. 10 For with the heart one believes unto righteousness, and with the mouth confession is made unto salvation. 13 For whoever calls on the name of the Lord shall be saved."

### 1 Corinthians 5:17-20 (NKJV)

17 "Therefore, if anyone is in Christ, he is a new creation; old things have passed away; behold, all things have become new. 18 Now all things are of God, who has reconciled us to Himself through Jesus Christ, and has given us the ministry of reconciliation, 19 that is, that God was in Christ reconciling the world to Himself, not imputing their trespasses to them, and has committed to us the word of reconciliation. 20 Now then, we are ambassadors for Christ, as though God were pleading through us: we implore you on Christ's behalf, be reconciled to God."

***Romans 12:1-2 (NKJV)***

*1 "I beseech you, therefore, brethren, by the mercies of God, that you present your bodies a living sacrifice, holy, acceptable to God, which is your reasonable service. 2 And do not be conformed to this world, but be transformed by the renewing of your mind, that you may prove what is that good and acceptable and perfect will of God."*

# CHAPTER 2

## *Who Am I Now?*

Woman of God, you have to find out and know who God is first in order to know who you are. You were made in His image and after His likeness. When He made you, He said you were good and very good. You are perfectly and wonderfully made by God. He was with you while you were in your mother's womb, fashioning your days for you and writing them in His book when you didn't have days that even existed yet.

God wants to have a relationship with you. He sees you and loves you as His child. He wants you to know Him as your Heavenly Father. He is King of Kings and Lord of Lords. He wants you to return to Him, who is your first love. Ask God what His plans, purpose, and destiny are for you. Then, be willing to wait on, trust in and believe in Him to receive all that He has in store for you. While on this journey that God has you on, be willing to be still in His presence so He can speak, you can hear and obey His direction and guidance. In doing so, by faith with His grace upon you, He will enable you to do exactly all that He has for you to do for His glory. It is in Jesus that we have a future and a hope.

One thing that I have learned while on this journey that God has me on with Him, is that I no longer have to compromise or settle for anything that I feel is not good for me to get involved in. I had to learn the hard way to be more of a God pleaser instead of a man and a woman pleaser. When I didn't know who I was in Christ Jesus and I didn't have a relationship with Him, I was looking for somebody to really love me like I felt I needed to be loved. I tried to do whatever I needed to do to receive love from people and to seek their approval of me. I discovered the difference between real unconditional love and fake conditional love early in life. It is not a healthy relationship when you can't say no to a person when they want you to do something that you don't feel comfortable doing or that is wrong for you to do – no matter if it is a man or a woman. What may be alright for some people to do may not be alright for you to do.

I had a hard time saying no when I needed to. I was grieved in my spirit, and my heart was broken many times because I didn't say no. I was constantly seeking love that I felt I wasn't getting. I was looking for love in all of the wrong places.

I want you to know this, when a child doesn't get unconditional love from home, they will seek it elsewhere. Do you know why? God is love, and He made us in His image and after His likeness. Therefore, we want to receive love and give love. Praise God. The day I gave my life to Jesus Christ is when I discovered just how much God really loves me. All the love I was looking for was always there. I have the unconditional agape love from God. He loved me so much that He saved me! I was lost and now I'm found.

When you learn who you are and whom you belong to, you will then try the spirit by the Spirit. Learn how to acknowledge God in all of your ways, and He will direct your path. If it is God's Spirit that is directing and guiding you, then you will experience "peace which surpasses all understanding that will guard your heart and your mind through Christ Jesus." If you don't feel that inner peace that can only come from Christ Jesus, then you will know that is not God. Then you will make a righteous decision not to get involved in whatever it is that the enemy (Satan) is trying to get you to get involved in.

It is in Jesus that we have a future and a hope. It is in Jesus that He can bring us into our expected end that He has planned for us. So take your journey with Jesus Christ. Then you will find out exactly who you are.

### *Jeremiah 29:11 (NKJV)*
*11 "For I know the thoughts that I think toward you, says the Lord, thoughts of peace and not of evil, to give you a future and a hope."*

### *Psalm 139:1-3, 13-18 (NKJV)*
*1 "O Lord, You have searched me and known me.*
*2 You know my sitting down and my rising up; You understand my thought afar off.*

*3 You comprehend my path and my lying down,
And are acquainted with all my ways.
13 For You formed my inward parts; You covered me in my mother's womb.
14 I will praise You, for I am fearfully and wonderfully made;
Marvelous are Your works,
And that my soul knows very well.
15 My frame was not hidden from You, When I was made in secret,
And skillfully wrought in the lowest parts of the earth.
16 Your eyes saw my substance, being yet unformed.
And in Your book they all were written, The days fashioned for me,
When as yet there were none of them.
17 How precious also are Your thoughts to me, O God! How great is the sum of them!
18 If I should count them, they would be more in number than the sand;
When I awake, I am still with You."*

## ***Philippians 4:6-7 (NKJV)***
*6 "Be anxious for nothing, but in everything by prayer and supplication, with thanksgiving, let*

*your requests be made known to God; 7 and the peace of God, which surpasses all understanding, will guard your hearts and minds through Christ Jesus."*

**Proverbs 3:5-6 (NKJV)**
*5 "Trust in the Lord with all your heart, and lean not on your own understanding; 6 In all your ways acknowledge Him, and He shall direct your paths."*

# CHAPTER 3

## *How To Experience A Spiritual Birth In Jesus Christ*

Godly women will support and defend the Word of God against opposition and/or criticism. From the beginning of time, women were made by God to give birth and to serve God and His people. Women were followers of Jesus Christ and helped to serve and support Him in His ministry while He was here on earth. Once a woman makes a righteous decision to give her life to Jesus and live for Him, she will not only be able to give birth to children but to the attributes, characteristics, and principles of God and His Word. Women can successfully do this by becoming devoted, loyal, and righteous followers of Jesus Christ. Godly women always put God first in their lives.

Godly women are receivers and are able to give birth to whatever God has impregnated into their spiritual womb. A spirit-filled woman of God becomes a holy righteous activist of the gospel of Jesus Christ, a servant and a doer of God's Word. A spirit-filled woman of God is able to develop, grow, and give form to every task that is required of her with wisdom to create the condition of the world around her. Since we are able to give a spiritual birth to what God has impregnated into our spiritual womb, let us also look at the difference and compare what it is like in giving birth to a baby in the natural sense. I'm getting ready to take you on a little journey with me, so get ready!

When I found out that I was pregnant with my first child, I was afraid because I had never experienced giving birth to a baby before, let alone raising a child. Not only that; but I almost miscarried him in my third month. I was put on complete bed rest until it was time for him to be born. I wanted so badly to have children that I was determined to do whatever I needed to do to make sure that my baby would be born healthy and normal. I was experiencing some trials and tribulations at that time. No matter what I was experiencing in my life; I knew that God is the giver of life and that my unborn child had a purpose in life for being born. I had to overcome any fears and put my trust totally and completely in God! I did this by reading His Word and praying. I would read the Bible out loud so that my baby would hear it as well. I would even lay my hands on my stomach and pray for him. In fact, I did that when I was pregnant with all three of my children.

I started going to Lamaze classes. I also learned in those classes that not only what I ate or drank would have an effect on my baby, but my thoughts and attitude would have an effect on my unborn child as well. I noticed when I would get upset that my stomach felt like it would ball up in a knot. My unborn baby didn't feel comfortable with how I was feeling either. So with God's help and guidance, I started really working on my attitude and thoughts. At the time, this was challenging for me, but I had to let go of any thoughts that I had been holding on to that were contrary to God and His Word.

I made up my mind that I didn't just have myself to think about, but I had my unborn baby to think about first. Like I said before, I wanted to give birth to a healthy, normal baby. Reading God's Word and listening to the gospel being preached and taught helped me in that area. I started listening to gospel music more and music that was soothing and pleasant for me to listen to. I read good inspirational books. I was mindful of what I even would watch as far as movies and TV programs. In other words, I had to guard my "gates" and not allow anything to enter through my eyes, ears, or heart that could enter into my unborn child as well.

I was told in Lamaze class that as soon as a child is conceived in the womb, the fetus (the baby) immediately attaches itself to the mother's bloodline in order to survive! While the unborn child is growing and developing inside the mother's womb, he/she is also attached to the umbilical cord. The umbilical cord is connecting the fetus (baby) with the placenta of the mother, transporting nourishment from the mother and wastes from the fetus (baby).

God is so awesome. Only He can do something that is as miraculous and powerful as conception and the process that a woman goes through in giving birth. It takes nine months for a baby to fully develop and grow in a woman's womb. Sometimes, women have given birth to a baby before the nine-month period, which is called premature birth. Even if a baby is born prematurely, the baby can still be born healthy and normal. Stay with me now! Are you still on this journey with me?

When I was pregnant for the first time, people started telling me that when you are in labor, death passes over you. Say what?? What does that mean? You mean to tell me that not only is a woman pregnant and feeling a human being growing inside of her for almost a year, but she's going to feel as if she's dying too?

Please don't listen to everything that people have to say to you! There can be some truth to what they are saying, but it is the way that they tell you. Especially to someone like me who had never given birth to a child before. Yes, your body does go through a metamorphosis when you're pregnant. In my opinion, a pregnant woman is absolutely beautiful. Yes, you may go through some mood swings. Just know that God is the giver of life, and you are not alone. He has you and your unborn child in His ever-loving hands and heart. He has a plan for every child that is born in this world. Knowing the joy that you experience holding your baby for the first time after giving birth, outweighs any discomfort you had during pregnancy and giving birth to your baby.

Finally, the day came for my baby to be born. I was experiencing so many mixed emotions. I was happy and excited because I wanted children so much. Then, on the other hand, I was very afraid because after all, this was my first time giving birth to a child. What an experience in giving birth. I had some complications, but I remembered what I had learned in Lamaze class and that really helped me. There is a reason they tell you to breathe a certain way instead of screaming and hollering. They told me that when the contractions come and you start screaming and hollering, your stomach muscles will tighten up and it is harder for the baby to push through the birth canal. Also, I learned in Lamaze class that when a woman starts having contractions her body automatically starts pushing the baby through her birth canal. Her breathing and pushing the correct way helps the birthing process.

Now, hospitals are allowing what they call coaches in the delivery room with the mother while she is giving birth to her baby. These coaches are in the delivery room to bring comfort and to help the mother to breathe, push or whatever is needed to help bring the unborn child into the world. Some of these coaches have experienced birthing a child before. Some may have even attended the Lamaze classes to prepare them for the birthing of the child. Either way, the mother and the unborn child are not alone and have all the support they need in the delivery room. The coaches can be the father of the unborn child, the grandparents of the unborn child or even a friend of the parents of the unborn child. Sometimes there may be complications that God has given doctors and nurses knowledge on how to help the mother stay healthy during the birthing process so that she can give birth to a healthy baby.

Experiencing a spiritual birth in Jesus Christ, in my opinion, is similar in a lot of ways to giving birth to a baby in the natural sense. When you first give your life to Jesus Christ, a lot of changes start happening that you were not even expecting. Your life, body, mind, soul, and spirit go through a metamorphosis! Yes, you become a new creature in Christ Jesus. You become so excited and happy. You want to tell everybody that you are saved, sanctified, and filled with God's Holy Spirit.

Salvation is a free gift from God, but it is not a feeling; it is a fact. You soon find out that your old sinful nature inside of you doesn't want to let you go. Your old sinful carnal-minded nature and your new spirit man in Jesus Christ are at war with each other. Keep in mind that once you've given your life over to Jesus, you are no longer a slave to sin. The battle is no longer yours, but God's. He has never lost a battle and never will.

We have to change our old way of thinking and our old way of living so the new birth of Jesus Christ can be born and come forth from the spirit man within us. Light has nothing to do with darkness. We must deny ourselves, pick up our crosses and follow after Jesus. He is the author and finisher of our faith. He is our bright and morning star and the keeper of our souls.

For Jesus Christ to be Lord and King in your life means that you want Him to have full control over your life. It means that you know that your life no longer belongs to you to do what you want to do. Your life now belongs to

God. It doesn't happen overnight either. It's just like a woman carrying a baby in her stomach for nine months. It is a process.

I had to stop hanging around the people I was hanging around with. I couldn't listen to them on how they thought I should continue to live. I wanted to make Jesus Christ my Lord, Savior, and King. I couldn't make Jesus Christ my Lord, Savior, and King if I continued to do some of the things that I was doing. I couldn't listen to the music I was listening to, watch the movies I was watching, and continue using substances that I thought would make me feel better about myself. Over the years, I made mistakes and asked God to forgive me. I'm still crying loud and sparing not to God, letting Him know how much I need Him to help me to live the life that pleases Him. I had to realize that I could no longer just think about myself anymore. I represent who Jesus Christ is in me.

Reading and meditating on His Word and hearing the Gospel being preached and taught is the only way we will be able to give birth to God's purpose and plans that He has for us. Everything we need to know on how God wants us to live a life that is pleasing in His sight is in

His Word. Every answer to all of our questions is in God's Word. God's Word is a lamp unto our feet and a light to our paths. Every trial and tribulation that we go through, God is there to deliver us and bring us out of all of them, if we just trust Him.

So, are you ready to experience a spiritual birth in Jesus Christ? If you haven't already, now is the time for you to go into your secret closet in prayer and ask God to come into your heart, forgive you and save you from all of your sins. Thank God for all that He has done for you. Let God know how much you love and need Him. Prayer is a very important part of the spiritual birthing process. It is like being in the delivery room when a woman is getting ready to give birth to her baby. As I mentioned before, I was taught in Lamaze class about not screaming and hollering when giving birth to my baby because it would prolong the birthing process. Don't complain when you are going through trials, tribulations, disappointments, hurts and pain. If you do, it will also prolong you giving birth to your destiny and purpose that God has impregnated you with in your spiritual womb.

I know it can be hard not to complain when it appears you are going through so much. Instead, just start calling on the name of Jesus. Praise Him and give Him all the glory, honor, and praise that He deserves. Don't pray the problems. When you murmur and complain, it stops the birthing of the great blessings that God has for you. Pray the solutions with God's Word, which is your weapon. Call those things into being as though they were. So while you bear down, crying loud and sparing not with praise and worship to God, know that you are not alone in giving birth to what God has impregnated you with.

You will have peace and enjoy the victorious life God has planned for you when God the Father, God the Son, and God the Holy Spirit are there with you telling you when and how to breathe with the breath of life they have given you. When you allow them to do so, you will experience the spiritual birth of Jesus Christ that is in you and your spirit man will dominate your flesh. Woman of God, don't stop pushing. Don't stop pressing and don't stop praising and calling on the name of Jesus. There are blessings in your pressing and pushing. Your coaches are right there with you through every step of the way to help you give birth to your destiny and purpose. Thank you Jesus! Praise the Lord!

### *Philippians 1:19-21 (NKJV)*
*19 "For I know that this will turn out for my deliverance through your prayer and the supply of the Spirit of Jesus Christ, 20 according to my earnest expectation and hope that in nothing I shall be ashamed, but with all boldness, as always, so now also Christ will be magnified in my body, whether by life or by death. 21 For to me, to live is Christ, and to die is gain."*

### *2 Corinthians 5:16-19 (NKJV)*
*16 "Therefore, from now on, we regard no one according to the flesh. Even though we have known Christ according to the flesh, yet now we know Him thus no longer. 17 Therefore, if anyone is in Christ, he is a new creation; old things have passed away; behold, all things have become new. 18 Now all things are of God, who has reconciled us to Himself through Jesus Christ, and has given us the ministry of reconciliation, 19 that is, that God was in Christ*

*reconciling the world to Himself, not imputing their trespasses to them, and has committed to us the word of reconciliation."*

# CHAPTER 4

## *Characteristics of A Godly Woman*

The godly woman, whether single or married, is able to do exploits by living and adhering to the spiritual principles in the Word of God under the guidance and direction of the Holy Spirit. In her doing so, the godly woman will discover that these spiritual principles will not only change and impact her life, but everyone else who is a part of her life as well. When observing the characteristics of a godly woman in Proverbs 31, we see that by applying these spiritual principles, the Proverbs 31 woman was able to live a peaceful, prosperous, and enjoyable life for her and her family. With time and effort, she realizes that under God's grace and protection, all her abilities to meet every task with strength and wisdom come from God.

The godly woman has control over her spirit and is a good manager and caregiver in her home.

The godly woman is a leader that leads by example. She stands firm in her beliefs, and she governs her life according to the truths and principles in God's Word. The godly woman has a holy, reverent fear of the Lord. She respects, obeys, and honors Him as her Lord, Savior, and King. By being obedient to the Word of God, the needs of the godly woman are met according to God's riches in glory by Christ Jesus.

I had to learn not to compromise the standards that God had given me to keep. When I get off track, God corrects and puts me right back on track again. I want Him to. God showed me how to set boundaries in my home and my life, even with my children and other family members. When you learn that you can't please everybody and everybody can't please you, then it becomes much easier for you to adhere to the spiritual principles in the Word of God. Our homes and our lives belong to God. What God says is right is right, and what He says is wrong is wrong. Keep in mind that, as a godly woman, God may tell you to do something that He may not tell someone else to do and vice versa.

The godly woman always strives to live a life that is pleasing to God. Whatever she finds for her hands to do, she does it to glorify God and Him alone! There is no glory in her flesh for she realizes to live is Christ, and to die is gain.

**2 Corinthians 12:9 (NKJV)**
*9 "And He said to me, "My grace is sufficient for you, for My strength is made perfect in weakness." Therefore most gladly I will rather boast in my infirmities, that the power of Christ may rest upon me."*

**Proverbs 31:25-29 (NKJV)**
*25 "Strength and honor are her clothing;
She shall rejoice in time to come.
26 She opens her mouth with wisdom,
And on her tongue is the law of kindness.
27 She watches over the ways of her household,
And does not eat the bread of idleness.
28 Her children rise up and call her blessed;
Her husband also, and he praises her:
29 "Many daughters have done well,
But you excel them all."*

**Proverbs 31:13-19 (NKJV)**

*13 "She seeks wool and flax, And willingly works with her hands.*
*14 She is like the merchant ships,*
*She brings her food from afar.*
*15 She also rises while it is yet night,*
*And provides food for her household,*
*And a portion for her maidservants.*
*16 She considers a field and buys it;*
*From her profits she plants a vineyard.*
*17 She girds herself with strength,*
*And strengthens her arms.*
*18 She perceives that her merchandise is good,*
*And her lamp does not go out by night.*
*19 She stretches out her hands to the distaff,*
*And her hand holds the spindle."*

***Proverbs 31:20-24 (NKJV)***

*20 "She extends her hand to the poor,*
*Yes, she reaches out her hands to the needy.*
*21 She is not afraid of snow for her household,*
*For all her household is clothed with scarlet.*
*22 She makes tapestry for herself;*
*Her clothing is fine linen and purple.*
*23 Her husband is known in the gates,*
*When he sits among the elders of the land.*

*24 She makes linen garments and sells them,
And supplies sashes for the merchants."*

# CHAPTER 5

## *Characteristics of A Godly Wife*

A woman of God must first be content with being a bride of Christ. Once you have given your life to Jesus Christ, you are considered His bride. Jesus Christ is your bridegroom, and He's coming back for a church without spot or wrinkle. The church is actually you and not a building made with the hands of man. When you realize and believe what the Word of God says in Isaiah 54:5 that God your Maker is your husband, then God will always be the head of your household. In fact, when you are single and believing God for a husband, ask God to manifest Himself as a husband in your life. Be ready when He does answer your prayers.

When a godly man finds a wife, he finds a good thing and obtains favor from the Lord. When he finds her, exactly what does he find her doing? I said a godly man – a man that has the love of God full in his heart. A man that desires to worship, praise, serve, and live for the Lord in Spirit and in truth. So when a godly man finds his wife, he is being led by the Holy Spirit! He is looking for a godly woman that is already serving the Lord. He is actually looking for what God intended and created for a man and a woman from the beginning of time. He is looking for his helpmeet, his rib. There is nothing too hard or impossible with God.

If you and your husband are not saved before you are married, then God can still save you both, if you just keep praying, obeying, and trusting God. Just make sure you are being led by the Holy Spirit. Marriage takes work for both the husband and wife. Allowing God to be in control and in charge of your marriage and following the principles for marriage in God's Word is the key to a successful marriage.

For you to be a submissive godly wife, you have to learn how to submit or yield to the authority of each other with humility and obedience. If you don't learn how to be submissive to God first and obey Him, don't think that you will be successful in being a submissive wife to your husband either. There are no perfect people in this world. We are all striving for perfection. Jesus Christ is the only one that is perfect. So since you are not perfect, stop expecting your husband to be. Wives, learn how to stay in your lane. You don't have the power to change anybody. Pray for your husband that God will have His way and will direct his life. Pray! Lord, let it be done according to your Word for my husband, for Your Glory, Lord in Jesus' name!

Be mindful that the order of your house should be God first, husband second, children and grandchildren third, and ministry and helping others fourth. Why? Think about the creation. God created the heavens and earth. God created man first, then from his rib, He created woman and then from woman came children and grandchildren. God had order and everyone had a place in His creation. He made sure with all His infinite wisdom that everything was in place and created a beautiful home, the Garden of Eden, for Adam and his family to live in. He gave Adam instructions for him and his family to follow. In other words, God being the owner of all His creation, made Adam the manager of all His creation.

Unfortunately, sin entered into this world through Adam disobeying God's commands and his wife, Eve, being deceived by the enemy, Satan. What happened? They got out of their place and lane from the order that God had given. Adam was right there when Eve was being tempted by the enemy's lies and deceit. He didn't stop her and took the fruit from the tree of knowledge of good and evil when his wife offered it to him. You already know that when God created everything, He said it was good and very good. So Adam was probably so overwhelmed by Eve's beauty that he probably forgot all about what God had told him. I guess we may find out what really happened when we get to heaven.

Communication is very important in a marriage. A lack of communication can cause a big problem. Eve should have turned to her husband Adam and said, "Husband, what do you think about what this serpent is saying to me and telling me to do?" Or, "Adam, what did God tell you about this tree?"

Adam, being the head and covering for his wife, should have rebuked that serpent and sent him back from whence he came. Then, Adam should have explained to his wife, Eve, what the Lord had commanded them to do. Like I said, Adam and Eve were not following the orders given by God, nor were they staying in their place and in their lane. There was no communication at all. Sounds like the lust of the eye and the pride of life was going on. I'm not judging at all and don't have a Heaven or Hell to put anyone in. Like I stated before, I'm still a work in process myself. I'm just making a point. I know, like us, Adam and Eve have been forgiven as well for their sins. Jesus came and paid the price on the cross for all of our sins. That doesn't mean that we are to continue to keep practicing sin.

Wives, don't use your body to get what you think you want from your husband. Stop using your body as a weapon to get what you want from him. In other words when you don't get what you want from your husband when you want it, then you refuse to show any love and affection to him with your body. You refuse to make love to him or allow him to make love to you. Yes, I said make love not have sex. When a husband and wife come together to make love to each other, the bed is not defiled. They are glorifying God. God is the One that instituted marriage, family, and relationships. Remember, you are one body, not two, right? Your body doesn't belong to you. It belongs to your husband, and his body belongs to you.

Of course, there are legitimate reasons why a husband and wife will not be able to be intimate with each other such as sickness, terminal illnesses, being in the hospital or even having to travel. When a married couple is not faced with these situations, then they should not refrain from being intimate with each other without consent. The principles of marriage concerning this matter are found in 1 Corinthians 7:1-5 NKJV and it reads as follows:

*"1 Now concerning the things of which you wrote to me: It is good for a man not to touch a woman. 2 Nevertheless, because of sexual immorality, let each man have his own wife, and let each woman have her own husband. 3 Let the husband render to his wife the affection due her, and likewise also the wife*

*to her husband. ⁴ The wife does not have authority over her own body, but the husband does. And likewise the husband does not have authority over his own body, but the wife does. ⁵ Do not deprive one another except with consent for a time, that you may give yourselves to fasting and prayer; and come together again so that Satan does not tempt you because of your lack of self-control."*

Let's take a look at The Song of Solomon in the Bible. Why believe and read some of the Bible, but not all of the Bible? Song of Solomon 1:2 says, *"Let him kiss me with the kisses of his mouth for your love is better than wine."* Song of Solomon 1:15-16 says, ¹⁵*"Behold, you are fair my love! Behold you are fair! You have dove eyes!"* ¹⁶*"Behold you are handsome, my beloved! Yes pleasant! Also, our bed is green!"* Woman of God, this is in the Bible that God put there Himself for godly husbands and wives to abide and live by. There are other scriptures in the Bible for husbands and wives to live by. These are not my words. By all means, read the Song of Solomon and other scriptures in the Bible for yourself. God is still leading me to read scriptures that I needed to read myself. So I'm sharing in this book what He is guiding me to share. I'm just the messenger.

There is one other message God wants me to give concerning marriage. Whatever goes on between you and your husband is nobody's business. I'm talking about personal business. Sometimes we talk a little too much. Okay, let me make it as real and plain as possible. Whatever goes on between you and your husband in the privacy of your home and bedroom should not be discussed with anyone. Not even your family. If there is something that you would like for your husband to do to please you, discuss it with him, and he should do the same with you. One time, I had someone come to me talking about her husband in a very bad way. I didn't feel comfortable about what I was hearing. I felt it wasn't any of my business. When people come to you to try to discuss their personal business about their marriage, stop them, and tell them that it is none of your business and shouldn't be discussed.

A lot of times women tell their business to you hoping that you will tell yours. If you start talking about how your husband is with you in the privacy of your home and bedroom, then whoever you are telling it to will start looking at your husband in a different way. That is something you may regret and don't want to happen. I'm not saying anything would happen if you did, but again, it is nobody's business.

Be careful what you keep listening to as well. Sometimes people have no intention of changing their ways or environment. They just want to use you as a sounding board. Trust me. They are not going to leave their husband at all. Please don't get me wrong. Sometimes we need someone that we can vent to, that we know will not judge but give us wise counsel and pray for us. If that be the case, ask God to show you who that person can be. Know that you can always go to God to tell Him about your troubles. He is the best counselor you could ever have. So, of course always go to Him before anyone else.

I have learned from other wise women of God how to live as a godly wife. There was an older woman that I had in my life years ago that was truly a mighty woman of God. She was like a mother to me. In fact, I called her mother with her last name afterwards. She went to church faithfully and was very active in ministry. She was about her Father God's business. Unfortunately, her husband was not saved. After they had been married for 26 years, he got into an adulterous affair and left her. This is not the first time I had ever heard of something like that happening in a marriage. It was different this time though.

Mother came to me and told me these words that have stayed with me over the years. She said, "Whatever you do, make sure you spend time with your husband. I didn't like I should have. I was in church all the time during the week and all day on Sunday. I made sure he had something to eat and would leave and go back to church. Don't make the same mistake I did. Because you are one flesh and not two, make God first and your husband second. Everything and everybody comes after that!" She never spoke badly of him at all.

After she finished talking to me, I was thanking God for having such an awesome woman of God in my life who showed me an example of how a woman of God should be to her husband. Sometimes we can learn from other people's experiences. She also showed me how to forgive. I will never forget Mother.

Years ago, someone gave me a cassette tape of a message that an evangelist had given at a women's conference. Unfortunately, it was so long ago I can't even remember her name, but I sure remember the message. It was so profound that one day I played it for the women that attended the ministry, "Women Living for Jesus in Victory," that I was having in my home. The message that the evangelist gave in the tape was, "If your husband is not saved yet and has not given his life to Jesus Christ, don't start laying biblical brochures and booklets all over the house for him to read. Stop quoting scriptures to him all the time. Your body is the temple of the Holy Spirit. If your husband isn't saved and filled with God's precious Holy Spirit, then bring your husband to the body!"

You follow your husband as your husband follows Christ. I had been single for so long and had a hard time submitting to anybody. Especially since my first husband was controlling and abusive. I had to come to that realization and learn for myself how to follow my husband as he followed Christ. I had to let go of my past experiences in being married and receive what the Lord had in store for me.

Woman of God, start praying what the Word of the Lord says over yourself on how a wife should be to her husband. Study the Word of God on how a marriage should be and how a husband and wife should be to each other. Pray the Word, woman of God. Declare out of your mouth with faith that you and your husband are one flesh, not two, equally yoked and on one accord in every area of your relationship and marriage. So woman of God, don't allow the enemy to deceive you. Pray for you and your husband's marriage and remember there is death and life in the power of your tongue.

Now, just rest in God and wait for Him to do the finished work and bless your marriage beyond your expectations.

### *Isaiah 54:4-5 (NKJV)*

*4 "Do not fear, for you will not be ashamed. Neither be disgraced, for you will not be put to shame. For you will forget the shame of your youth and will not remember the reproach of your widowhood anymore. 5 For your Maker is your husband. The LORD of hosts is His name; and your Redeemer is the Holy One of Israel. He is called the God of the whole earth."*

***Ephesians 5:22-23 (NKJV) Marriage—Christ and the Church***
*22 "Wives, submit to your own husbands, as to the Lord. 23 For the husband is head of the wife, as also Christ is head of the church; and He is the Savior of the body."*

***Ephesians 5:25-27 (NKJV)***
*25 "Husbands, love your wives, just as Christ also loved the church and gave Himself for her, 26 that He might sanctify and cleanse her with the washing of water by the word, 27 that He might present her to Himself a glorious church, not having spot or wrinkle or any such thing, but that she should be holy and without blemish."*

***Hebrews 13:4 (NKJV)***
*4 "Marriage is honorable among all, and the bed undefiled; but fornicators and adulterers God will judge."*

***Revelation 19:7-8 (NKJV)***
*7 "Let us be glad and rejoice and give Him glory, for the marriage of the Lamb has come, and His wife has made herself ready. 8 And to her it was granted to be arrayed in fine linen, clean and*

*bright, for the fine linen is the righteous acts of the saints."*

**Proverbs 18:21-22 (NKJV)**
*21 "Death and life are in the power of the tongue and those who love it will eat its fruit. 22 He who finds a wife finds a good thing and obtains favor from the Lord."*

# CHAPTER 6

## Characteristics of A Godly Mother

*Mother: someone who exercises protective care and unconditional love over someone; to assume as one's own; to care for and protect.*

A woman doesn't have to give birth to a child to be a mother. God made a woman to give birth to hope, love, faith, joy, and peace to His people. A woman of God has the ability to give unconditional love to all those that God places in her life. God has placed people in my life that are children and adults younger than me that I love dearly. I know they love me, and I didn't give birth to them either. Some of them call me Mama Lauren, Mama Triplett, or Ma. At first, I didn't understand why people started calling me that, but I embraced and received it all with great joy and happiness. God enlarged my family and has given me more people to love.

God gives instructions in His Word to a godly mother to be a woman of wisdom, courage, and strength. The godly mother totally depends on God to be a leader that leads her children by example. She teaches them to live a life that is pleasing in God's sight and to wear the world as a loose garment, so that the world would not do them any harm. She gives wise counsel and is willing to give support and understanding when needed. A good counselor is not always one that has something to say but is one that is willing to listen to her children.

After listening to her children, she is guided by the Holy Spirit on what to say to them. I'm not going to say that this is easy to do all the time. Especially when you sense that your children are saying something or living in a way that you feel can bring them hurt and/or harm. It takes the grace of God to help you not to say or do something yourself that you will regret later.

A lot of times when I thought that way about my own children, I would immediately get in the protective mode like a mama bear and I ended up doing or saying something wrong. The outcome was not good at all, which was not my intention. I allowed my flesh and emotions to get in the way instead of seeking God first for His wisdom in the matter on how He wanted me to handle the situation. I had to repent to God and ask my children for forgiveness. Yes, I did. I realized that they belong to God, not me. I was a vessel for God to bring them into this world. God told me it's not what you say but how you say it. It's not what you do but how you do it. I meant what I told them, but I said it in a way that they did not receive it at all. When it comes to a godly mother's children, she represents God in everything that she says and does concerning them.

I have given birth to three sons. All three of them are truly a blessing to me. I thank God for them. I was so excited about being able to have my three precious children, especially when I didn't think I would be able to have children at all. I have experienced some horrific tragedies in my life that made me feel that way. Even my first marriage was an abusive relationship. That's another story and another time. God's love, grace and mercy brought me through them all. My God didn't only bless me to give birth to my children, but He blessed me to marry a mighty man of God. Regardless to any life challenges we may have experienced; we both raised our children together with the love of God. There is hope, woman of God. Praise God from whom all blessings flow.

I discovered early that even though I had given birth to three children, they were all different. They had some similarities, but they also had their own individual personalities. So it is important to know that when you have more than one child that you are raising in your home, they are going to be different. Whether you have given birth to them or not, love them unconditionally and treat them as individuals. Don't compare one child with the other. When you try to make a child feel like they have to think or act like their siblings, they will start feeling inadequate. They will feel they will never get your approval of anything that they set out to do in life. They will have low self-esteem and start doing things out of character just to get your attention.

Even a woman that has multiple births realizes that each child is born with their own fingerprints. God is so awesome. Even though we were made in His image and after His likeness, He made us all with different fingerprints. He purposely made us all different. He said in His Word that He made us all "good and very good." In spite of our differences, God loves us unconditionally. Knowing that God is our Heavenly Father and we are His children, then we should love all the children that God has blessed us with the same way even in our children's differences.

As a godly mother, when raising your children with the Lord, they go through different stages of growth and maturity. You go through those stages with them. They start as babies, then teenagers, young adults, and then full-grown adult children. Then you end up saying, "Wow! Where did the time go?"

I tell people with children to enjoy them while you can because before you know it, they will be gone from under your roof and living their own lives. My mother-in-law would always give me sound wisdom on how to raise our children. We call her Granny Triplett. She would say, "When your children are young, you can hold them in your hand, but when they get older you have to hold them in your heart." She would also say, "Tell your children to pick their friends and not let their friends pick them. God is in charge. He is in control."

Now, that was definitely wisdom speaking from God.

From my own experience, I've learned that when your children become adults, you have to allow them to live out their own life testimonies just like we had to. That is why it is so important to train up your children in the way that they should go so that when they grow old, they will not depart from it. You want them not to depart from God.

Trust me, when your children become adults and you have raised them with the Lord, they are going to want to move away and live their own lives. I already knew that was bound to happen. But was I ready for them to go? No, I wasn't.

I had mixed emotions all over again! God had to remind me who they belonged to again. God even told me, one day when I was in His presence, that our children wouldn't be able to live the life that He had planned for them if they stayed under our roof.

I knew then that God was going to move them away from home. I didn't know when or how, but I knew it was coming. Sure enough, they all moved away from home, and I cried when each one did. Whether it was for college and/or to just experience life, they were all gone.

For the first time, my husband and I experienced what it was like to have an empty nest. Of course, their father loved and missed them, but he handled them leaving a little different than I did. He had to comfort me because I was a basket case at first. They visited us and we stayed in touched as much as possible, but it just wasn't the same for me. Now this was another lesson for me to learn of letting go and letting God be in total and complete control in our sons' lives. We enjoy them even more now when we come together as a family.

One day, I was praying and crying out to God about my sons. I could tell they were going through some challenges in their lives. I mean I was really praying a real deep prayer! I pleaded the blood of Jesus, came against the attack of the enemy and all his demons on my children and cast down strongholds. I was crying, spitting and calling on the name of Jesus over them! Then I started hollering, "Lord, I trust you." And I kept saying, "Lord, I trust you!!"

All of a sudden, I heard God say to me, "THEN STOP SAYING IT AND DO IT!!"

I immediately stopped praying, wiped my eyes and said, "Yes, Lord!"

God is not impressed by how deep and loud we pray. He wants us to be effective with our prayers. I've gotten a lot better now with my adult children living their own lives, but God had to help me overcome being able to let them go. Now when I pray for them, I pray, "Lord, let it be done unto them according to your Word, way, will, purpose and plan that you have for them."

Now, let me share one of my experiences that I had of letting go with one of our sons.

A few years ago, one of our sons decided he wanted to move to another country. That's right, I said another country. Meaning he would not only no longer live in the same city or state as we did but he would no longer live in the same country, the United States of America, as we did. He felt this was the journey he needed to take to fulfill his dreams in the career he had chosen. He even told me that he felt that God was leading him to move to another country. What could I say behind him saying that to me? The day that he told me what his plans were, I was careful how I reacted. I didn't want to say the wrong thing to him. Like I stated earlier, when I used to do that with my adult children, the end results were never good. I wanted to scream to him, "NOOOOOO!!"

That was too far away from us! I held my peace with him and said I would pray for him. I always pray for God's will and way to be done in my children's lives. Even though I was careful with what I said to him at that time, I was very upset to the point that I could hardly go to sleep that night. But then I finally fell asleep.

The Lord woke me up the next morning and I heard him tell me to get my Life Application Study Bible. God told me to read about Mary, the mother of Jesus and what she had to experience in having to let go of her son. Mary, the mother of Jesus had to experience some things that none of us will ever have to experience as a mother. Her son, Jesus Christ was the Son of God. Her son, Jesus, was conceived by the Holy Spirit. She was a virgin when she got pregnant. With me knowing this,

I couldn't understand why God wanted me to read and study that again.

To me, at the time, reading about Mary and Jesus had nothing to do with my son wanting to move to another country miles away from us. After all, I couldn't top what Mary did anyway. I wasn't a virgin at all when my three sons were conceived. God spoke to me again and said, "Read it."

Why do we always want to reason with and question God like we know everything and He doesn't know what is best for us?

Needless to say, God led me to read Luke 2:41-52. I was obedient and read it. I would like to encourage you to read it as well. The passage of scripture is about when Jesus was just 12 years old and was traveling with His family to Jerusalem to the yearly Feast of the Passover. When His parents and family headed back home, Jesus decided at the age of 12 to stay in Jerusalem to listen and ask questions to the religious leaders there. The religious leaders were amazed at how this little 12-year-old boy was able to ask such advanced, mature, intelligent questions for His age. After traveling a day's journey, Jesus' parents, Mary and

Joseph, discovered that Jesus wasn't with them. Frantically, they looked for Jesus everywhere. When they found Him in Jerusalem, they were very upset and Mary asked Him, "Why did you do this to us Jesus? Don't you know, Jesus, that your father and I have sought you anxiously?"

Do you know how Jesus, at the age of 12, answered His mother? He said to Mary His mother, "Why do you seek me? Did you not know that I must be about my Father's business?"

In other words, Jesus reminded His mother who His Father really was. Jesus was on a mission, and He knew at a young age that His purpose and destiny for being born had to be fulfilled. Since God had me to read it in my study Bible, He then led me to read the footnotes at the bottom of the page.

When I read the footnotes, it was life changing. Again, I learned the more I study and meditate on God and His Word, the more I realize how much I don't know. I thank God for giving me a word of truth on how to trust Him concerning my children and to leave them in His hands. I would like to share with you what I read on that day. I have shared it with others as well. I hope this footnote will be a blessing to you as it has been to me on how a godly mother should be with all of her children.

The scripture footnote comes from Luke 2:48 and it reads as follows: ***"Mary had to let go of her child and let him become a man, God's Son, the Messiah. Fearful that she hadn't been careful enough with this God-given child, she searched frantically for him. But she was looking for a boy, not the young man who was in the temple astounding the religious leaders with his questions. Letting go of people or projects we have nurtured can be very difficult. It is both sweet and painful to see our children growing into adults, our students into teachers, our subordinates into managers, our inspirations into institutions. But when the time comes, we must step back and let go – in spite of the hurt. Then our protégés can exercise their wings, take flight, and soar to the heights God intended for them!"***

In closing of this chapter, (The Godly Mother), I would like to share a poem with you. I was inspired by the Holy Spirit to write this poem to my three sons. If you are a parent, then you will feel and be able to relate to what is coming from my heart as you read this poem.

## FROM MY HEART

I am thankful to God that I have given birth to a nation that was born with crowns
Even though I'm aware that there are gang slayers around
God is not finished with any of us yet
So be aware when you are chosen by God that you don't fall into the enemies' net

All gifts, talents, skills and abilities come from God alone
So in due time and season God will expose and let it be shown
Continue to not only let the real truth be told but let it be known
Don't let people hang around you with their false lies, opinions, and words
They want to try to take your crowns and steal the truth as you know it

Keep in mind the testimonies Dad and I have shared
Of all the heartaches, mistakes and failures we had to bear
Through it all, our God is good
His love, grace, peace and mercy brought us through
as we knew He could
Who the Son set free is free indeed
Just know, my sons, that no matter what or no matter who that you are all good seeds

A foundation of truth has been laid as you know it
With the truth being in you, let the words that you speak as a river flow in it
Not only with words but with your life being a living testimony
God is more concerned about bringing you into your destiny from your journey
No matter how many mistakes and failures you are going to make or you have made
Remember through the blood and love of our Lord and Savior Jesus Christ
A foundation of truth and freedom has been laid
I know and pray that your lives, destiny and purpose are in God's hands
Therefore, you will experience eating the good of the land

My sons, take God with you wherever you go
So in your calling you are victorious and will be able to grow
There is power in your spoken words and you are the words that you speak
When you speak words like a king with a crown
True words spoken are not words that will fall to the ground
I may not have gifts and talents like you as you can see
But from my heart has grown my three precious seeds

Written By: Lauren D. Triplett

# CHAPTER 7

## *Conclusion*

As Women Living for Jesus in Victory, we must always strive to live a life that is pleasing to God. Whatever we find for our hands to do, we do it to glorify God and Him alone. There is no glory in our flesh, for we realize that to live is Christ, to die is gain. As Women Living for Jesus in Victory, we have come to the conclusion that in living for Jesus Christ we no longer have to live a defeated life as a victim but we have an overcoming victorious life as MIGHTY WOMEN OF GOD!

**Isaiah 1:19 (NKJV)**
19 *"If you are willing and obedient, you shall eat the good of the land."*

***Proverbs 31:30-31 (NKJV)***

*30 "Charm is deceitful and beauty is passing, but a woman who fears the Lord, she shall be praised. 31 Give her of the fruit of her hands and let her own works praise her in the gates."*

# ABOUT THE AUTHOR

Lauren Triplett was ordained as a pastor, elder and leader over Strategic Governmental Prayer Ministry at New Breakthrough Church Intl. in Detroit, Michigan, under the leadership of Pastor Donald Coleman. After moving to North Carolina and joining Love and Faith Christian Fellowship, under the leadership of Pastor Michael Thomas, she has been actively involved in ministries there, such as, Healing and Restoration Ministry, Witnessing Ministry, and Ministers Class. She has also shared a word of encouragement to women at StepUp Greensboro Character Development as a facilitator and mentor. On occasion, Lauren has ministered to women at Daughters of Zion.

Lauren has been called to teach and preach the true unadulterated Word of God. Her passion is to minister to people who are abused, hurt, rejected, and lost. As an intercessor and prayer warrior, she teaches others how to bombard the gates of Hell by coming against the kingdom of darkness in spiritual warfare.

As a younger woman in her 20's, Lauren was ordained as an evangelist where she began preaching and teaching the Word of God. As time went on and with life experiences of abuse, rejection, looking for love in all the wrong places, finding ways to deal with her pain and low self-esteem, Lauren was propelled to start a women's ministry in her home. Under the anointing and power of God, through her teachings and prayers, women were healed, delivered, and set free.

From that ministry, God transitioned her into the church to minister to women and others that needed to be healed, delivered, and set free.

Lauren finds joy in worshipping, praising and glorifying God for who He is. He is the King of Kings and Lord of Lords in her life. He is her Savior and the keeper of her soul. God is not finished with her yet. She knows she's still a work in progress. She knows she still needs God in her life. What has made her the woman of God that she is today are her life experiences in the school of adversity.

Lauren attended Wayne State College of Lifelong Learning and Wayne County Community College. She studied biblical courses at the

Detroit Bible College, also known as William Tyndale College (now closed). She also attended New Breakthrough Church International School of Ministry. She held various positions in different aspects of office administration and childcare for over 20 years.

She has made a righteous decision to stay in relationship with God by obeying His Word and by embracing His will for her life. She is blessed to be married to a man of God, Milton Triplett. They raised their three sons Jason, Jonathan, and James to obey the Word of God and to live a holy righteous life.

# ORDER AND CONTACT INFORMATION

If you need to contact the author or order additional copies of *Women Living For Jesus In Victory,* please use the following email address:

laurendtriplett@gmail.com

Books are also available at Amazon.com, BN.com, and Kindle

www.ingramcontent.com/pod-product-compliance
Lightning Source LLC
Chambersburg PA
CBHW071157090426
42736CB00012B/2358